Chris Lee

Shallow Slumber

T0258366

Methuen Drama

Published by Methuen Drama 2012

Methuen Drama, an imprint of Bloomsbury Publishing Plc

1 3 5 7 9 10 8 6 4 2

Methuen Drama
Bloomsbury Publishing Plc
50 Bedford Square
London WC1B 3DP
www.methuendrama.com

First published by Methuen Drama in 2012

ISBN 978 1 408 17267 4

A CIP catalogue record for this book is available from the British Library

Available in the USA from Bloomsbury Academic & Professional, 175 Fifth
Avenue/3rd Floor, New York, NY 10010. www.BloomsburyAcademicUSA.com

Typeset by Mark Heslington Ltd, Scarborough, North Yorkshire

Ben Monks and Will Young for

supporting
wall

present

Shallow Slumber
by Chris Lee

World premiere at Soho Theatre, London,
on Tuesday 24 January 2012

Shallow Slumber
by Chris Lee

Cast

MOIRA   Alexandra Gilbreath
DAWN   Amy Cudden

Director	Mary Nighy
Set & costume designer	Georgia Lowe
Lighting designer	Christopher Nairne
Sound designer	Ed Borgnis
Voice coach	John Tucker
Fight adviser	Alison de Burgh
Casting director	Juliet Horsley
Set builder	Toby Albrow
Production assistant	Anastasiya Trayanova
Produced by	Ben Monks & Will Young for Supporting Wall

Production supported by the Royal Victoria Hall Foundation, Lord Ramsbotham and Lord Archer. With thanks to Giles Smart at United Agents; Nina Steiger, Steve Marmion and all at the Soho Theatre; Charlotte Loveridge at Methuen Drama; Nicholas Allott at Cameron Mackintosh; Thelma Holt; and Sir Stephen Waley-Cohen.

Supporting Wall Limited is a not-for-profit theatre company registered in England and Wales, number 7081594.

www.supportingwall.com

Chris Lee

Chris is an award-winning playwright and full-time social worker. He is a former Pearson Playwright-in-Residence at the Finborough Theatre (where plays include *The Optimist's Daughter, Online and Paranoid in the Sentimental City* and *Regolith*) and Associate Writer at Dublin's Abbey Theatre (where plays include *The Electrocution of Children*, winner of the Stewart Parker New Playwright's Award, and *The Map Maker's Sorrow*, both produced in the Peacock Theatre).

Chris has also won Bath's Rondo Theatre award (for *The Foundation of Trust*). Other plays include *Vermilion Dream* (Salisbury Playhouse), *The Water Harvest, The Ash Boy* (both at Theatre 503) and *Hummingbird* (Old Red Lion Theatre).

Mary Nighy

Mary trained at the National Film and Television School and in 2005 was named a UK Film Council Breakthrough Brit. Her film credits include shorts *Into the Night, Small Town Glory* and *Player* (starring Pete Postlethwaite); and the documentary *Convoy to Cape Town* for the White Ribbon Alliance. Previous theatre direction includes Megan Walsh's *Lyre* at the 2007 HighTide Festival.

Mary has also won acclaim as an actress for film roles including Sophia Coppola's *Marie Antoinette*, among others.

Alexandra Gilbreath

Trained at LAMDA, Alexandra was nominated for a 2010 Olivier Award for *Twelfth Night* (RSC) and won the 1996 Ian Charleson Award for *Hedda Gabler* (ETT).

Other theatre includes *Othello* (Sheffield Crucible), *The Village Bike* (Royal Court), *Hayfever* (The Rose, Kingston), *Merry Wives – The Musical, The Tamer Tamed, The Taming of the Shrew, As You Like It, Romeo and Juliet, The Winter's Tale, Cyrano de Bergerac* (all RSC), *Lucky You* (Magic Key Productions) and *The House of Bernada Alba* (Gate Theatre).

Television includes *Rights of Passage* (pilot for Company Productions), *Inspector George Gently* (Company Pictures), *Casualty* (BBC), *Trial & Retribution* (ITV), *Life Begins* (semi-regular for ITV), *Absolute Power* (BBC), *The Commander* (ITV), *The Waltz King* (BBC), *Happiness* (BBC), *Midsomer Murders* (ITV), *The Bill* (semi-regular for Thames), *The Project* (Ecosse Films), *Monarch of the Glen* (BBC), *Out of Hours* (BBC) and *A Wing and a Prayer* (Thames).

Film includes *Dead Babies* (Gruber Brothers).

Amy Cudden

Amy is a graduate of the Oxford School of Drama.

Recent television credits include *Phoneshop* (Channel 4), *Doctor Who* (BBC), *Vera* (ITV), *The Bill* (Talkback Thames) and *Casualty* (BBC).

Theatre includes *Plasticine* (Southwark Playhouse), *Crooked House* (Bad Physics/BAC) and *Woyzeck* (GBS Theatre).

Film includes *Deep Sleep*.

Georgia Lowe

Georgia trained on the Motley Theatre Design course and was a 2011 Linbury Prize finalist. She is a trainee designer with the RSC, and was previously resident designer at the Broadway Studio Theatre.

Recent design credits include *Fog* and *Blue Surge*, both directed by Che Walker (Finborough Theatre), *Amphibians* (Bridewell Theatre), *Yellow* (Supporting Wall/Tête à Tête: The Opera Festival 2011, Riverside Studios), *Fanny and Faggot* (Finborough Theatre, Pleasance Edinburgh & Trafalgar Studios) and *In My Name* (Trafalgar Studios). She is currently designing *The Dark Side of Love* (RSC World Shakespeare Festival).

Christopher Nairne

Previous credits for Supporting Wall include *The Jewish Wife* (BAC, JMK Award winner) and, as assistant LD, *Moonfleece* (London & tour). Previous credits at the Soho Theatre include *La Bohème* (OperaUpClose, 2011 Olivier Award winner).

Other recent lighting designs include *A Dish of Tea with Dr Johnson* (Out of Joint, UK tour & Arts Theatre), *The Belle's Stratagem* (Southwark Playhouse), *The Cunning Little Vixen* (Ryedale Festival Opera), *For Services Rendered* (Union Theatre) and *The Kissing-Dance* (Jermyn Street Theatre).

Cabaret includes numerous shows for Frisky and Mannish (including Lyric Theatre, Riverside Studios, Edinburgh Fringe & UK/international tours), Shlomo (Southbank Centre, Union Chapel & Edinburgh Fringe), Morgan & West (Edinburgh Fringe) and various burlesque troupes (including at the O2).

Full details and credits at www.christophernairne.co.uk.

Ed Borgnis

Ed studied engineering at Warwick University before beginning his career at a film production company in Birmingham.

Sound design includes *Our Brother David* (Watford Palace), *Tactical Questioning*, *A Walk in the Woods* (Tricycle), *Broken Glass* (Tricycle/West End), *Blind Date* & *27 Wagons Full of Cotton* (double bill, Riverside Studios), *The Last Five Years*, *Tick Tick Boom* (Notes from New York/Duchess Theatre), *A Real Humane Person Who Cares and All That* (Arcola), *Beyond the Pale* (Southwark Playhouse) and *Moonfleece* (Supporting Wall/London & tour).

Ed tours comedy acts including Chris Addison and Dave Gorman, and provides technical support for the BBC.

Supporting Wall

Supporting Wall was founded in 2008 by Ben Monks and Will Young, supported by a SOLT/TMA Stage One Bursary in 2009, and this year has been nominated for a second consecutive OffWestEnd 'Offie' Award for Best Producer.

Shows in 2011 included the smash hit premiere of Philip Ridley's *Tender Napalm* (Southwark Playhouse; touring and returning to London in 2012) and *Yellow* (Tête à Tête: The Opera Festival, Riverside Studios); and in 2010 included Ridley's *Moonfleece* (London & tour), JMK Award winner *The Jewish Wife* (BAC) and rapid-response political theatre event *Election Drama* (New Players). Supporting Wall has also managed and promoted UK and international tours for a range of clients.

For more information, visit www.supportingwall.com.

Shallow Slumber

For all social workers everywhere

Characters

Moira, *a social worker*
Dawn, *a mother*

There are gaps of many years between the three acts, so the actors must play across maturing identities.

The play works backwards in time.

Setting
One of our cities

Act One

The threshold of **Moira**'s *home.* **Dawn** *and* **Moira** *face each other. Long silence.*

Dawn   You look well.

Pause.

I mean you look older. But you look well.

Pause.

Don't you believe me?

Pause.

You're still an ugly bitch.

Moira   I thought it was you.

Dawn   I could see your mind working.

Moira   I'm not sure my mind does work any more.

Dawn   It's good to see you.

Moira   Why?

Dawn   I've been thinking about you.

Moira   What for?

Dawn   I didn't have much else to do.

Moira   How did you find me?

Dawn   It's very easy.

Moira   Is it?

Dawn   You haven't made any effort to hide yourself.

Moira   Why would I?

Dawn   No reason. No reason at all, only everyone can be found. And if you don't actively want to disappear then you can be found very easily. That's all.

Moira   Well, you found me.

Dawn   Yes.

Moira   Here I am.

Pause.

Dawn   It's exciting.

Moira   Exciting?

Dawn   To see you again.

Moira   Why?

Dawn   I haven't had much excitement.

Moira   Oh.

Dawn   Not that many things to think about.

Moira   No.

Dawn   So I thought about you.

Moira   Glad to be of service.

Dawn   I didn't ask anything of you. I just thought about you.

Pause.

Moira   I haven't thought. I mean not in a bad way, but I haven't thought of you.

Dawn   Of course.

Pause.

Dawn   I mean why would you?

Moira   Not for a long time.

Dawn   You needed to forget.

Moira   Maybe I did.

Dawn   It's alright. I don't expect. You know. I don't expect . . .

Pause.

Dawn   Anything.

Moira   Right.

Dawn   I just wanted to set eyes on you.

Moira   Yes.

Dawn   I wanted to know that you were . . . doing well.

Moira   Doing well?

Dawn   Not doing badly.

Moira   I'm doing OK.

Dawn   That's good.

Pause.

Dawn   That's good isn't it?

Moira   I suppose it is.

Dawn   And I'm . . .

Moira   Doing well too.

Dawn   Oh not that far.

Moira   No?

Dawn   I'm just beginning. I mean I might. Soon even.

Moira   Are you saying you've only just been . . .?

Dawn   Only just yes. Three days.

Moira   I see.

Dawn   Quite a change.

Moira   It must be.

Dawn   Everything's different.

Moira   Sure.

Dawn   I don't mean any harm.

Moira   I know.

Pause.

Dawn   Can I come in?

Moira   Is that a good idea?

Dawn   I don't think it's an idea at all. Is it?

Moira   I mean what good would it do?

Dawn   For you?

Moira   Yes for me.

Dawn   I just . . .

Moira   Don't be offended.

Dawn   I'm sorry.

Moira   Please.

Pause.

Dawn   Fuck.

Pause.

Moira   I can't.

Dawn   I've got somewhere to stay. That's not what this is about.

Moira   Fine.

Dawn   You used to be so . . .

Pause.

Moira   Stupid?

Dawn   No, no, no. Not that. Not that at all.

Pause.

Moira   Dawn.

Dawn   What?

Moira   Oh Jesus, Dawn.

Dawn   Compassionate.

Moira   That was years ago.

Dawn   You haven't changed.

Moira   Oh but I have.

Dawn   You want to have changed. But you haven't. I know that because I knew you. I knew you would never change.

Moira   I had to change Dawn. I had to keep my soul ticking over with some kind of belief. So I left a lot of rage behind me.

Pause.

Dawn   It's a good thing you haven't changed. It's a very good thing. It's the best thing of all. Compassionate.

Moira   You're bullying me. You always bullied me.

Dawn   I wanted to please you.

Moira   We fucked up.

Dawn   You see, you see? We. You see?

Moira   I'm trying to be kind.

Dawn   You are kind.

Moira   Look.

Pause.

Dawn   You need more time.

Moira   I do not need more time.

Dawn   I just want to sit down.

Moira   I have to protect . . .

Dawn   Protect against what?

Moira   Everything. I have a new life. I need to look after what I have.

Dawn   I . . .

Pause.

Moira   If I let you in it doesn't mean anything.

Dawn   I'm not asking for anything.

Moira   Perhaps.

Dawn   Just to sit down. Just for a while.

Moira   Just to sit down.

Pause. **Moira** *moves aside and* **Dawn** *comes in. They both sit down.*

Dawn   So here I am.

Moira   In my home.

Dawn   Yes, I never was before was I.

Moira   No.

Dawn   It's just an ordinary home.

Moira   What else would it be?

Dawn   Yes that was silly. Ordinary. But nice.

Moira   Thank you.

Dawn   Been here long?

Moira   Five years.

Dawn   On your own?

Moira   Mostly.

Dawn   I like the colour.

Moira   So do I.

Dawn   Your own home.

Moira   Where are you staying?

Dawn   I have a hostel. To start with. It's not bad.

Moira   Good.

Dawn   I'll get a rent deposit. You can't get council housing at all these days.

Moira   I know, it's impossible.

Dawn   If I cut off all my limbs I'll qualify for a bedsit.

Moira   That's not an exaggeration.

Dawn   Have you still got the fire?

Moira   The fire?

Pause.

Dawn   Injustice. Oppression. Does it still make you angry?

Moira   Sometimes.

Dawn   Good.

Moira   Not as often.

Dawn   Hard to keep up the energy levels.

Moira   Can't be apoplectic all the time.

Dawn   No.

Pause.

Moira   They have a contract with the council. The rent deposit landlords. It's more regulated than it was. Some of the properties are pretty good.

Dawn   I'm fine with it. Really.

Moira   I hope it works out.

Dawn   I'm sure it will.

Moira   And they're furnished.

Dawn   Yes, it saves a lot of time.

Moira   It's only a place to live. To sleep. This too. I don't feel sentimental about it.

Dawn   But you got to choose.

Moira   Yes. I worked hard. I saved up. I got to choose.

Dawn   I'm not complaining.

Pause.

Moira   Would you like a . . . cup of tea? Or coffee?

Dawn   Coffee?

Moira   Yes. If you want.

Dawn   I'd love a coffee.

Moira   OK.

Dawn   I'd fucking love a coffee Moira. Thanks.

Pause. **Moira** *slowly gets up and goes to make a coffee. This must happen onstage. We wait for the kettle to boil and the coffee is made, poured and taken to* **Dawn**. **Moira** *sits down with her own cup.*

Dawn   Thanks.

Moira   No problem.

Pause.

Dawn   You didn't ask.

Moira   Ask what?

Dawn   Milk and three sugars.

Moira   No I . . . no I didn't ask.

Dawn   You remembered.

Pause.

Dawn   Do you think you can start again? Do you think that's possible?

Moira   It has to be.

Dawn   Or is it all shit. Is it all just something they tell you so that you'll go and they can forget you?

Moira   No, I don't think it's shit. I think it's possible. Not easy but possible.

Dawn   I believe that too.

Moira   Good.

Dawn   But only if I hear someone else say it. Only if I hear you say it.

Moira   You have to break things down into simple steps. You have to organise that feeling of being overwhelmed. Then you can concentrate on one task at a time.

Pause.

A lot has happened.

Dawn   Of course it has.

Moira   I'm not the same. Neither are you.

Dawn   Well we couldn't be could we?

Moira   No.

Dawn   But the fundamentals.

Moira   Sometimes it's comforting to think that there's this essence that remains the same in people over the years. But we do change with experience, I don't think we even notice. We get weathered. It's not all bad. The voice you use to object to the world gets less shrill.

Pause.

Dawn   You're still . . . you know. You're still that person.

Moira   I know you want to believe that. But I was crushed. I couldn't decide what to do. I wondered what it would be like to be just about OK. Then I sort of tried to trace it back to the present. Tiny steps. It didn't feel like change at first, just getting through the day. But after a while, yes, I had started again.

Dawn   Yes.

Pause.

Dawn   But I think I'm right.

Moira   As ever.

Pause.

Dawn   I wanted your advice.

Moira   I gave a lot of advice in those days.

Dawn   I loved your advice.

Moira   Yes but you didn't take it.

Dawn   But that's not the point of advice is it?

Moira   Isn't it?

Dawn   No. Advice is about reassurance. Advice is just proof that you're listening. That's all.

Moira   Ah, so that's where I've been going wrong.

Pause.

Dawn   You never went back?

Moira   No.

Dawn   That's such a shame.

Moira   Once bitten.

Dawn   I know it was horrible.

Moira   Yes.

Dawn   For you I mean.

Moira   Yes.

Dawn   But it's in your blood.

Moira   Oh no no no.

Dawn   A gift.

Moira   A gift?

Dawn   Yes.

Moira   A curse.

Pause.

Dawn   Why is that so funny?

Moira   Just because of what happened.

Dawn   I didn't want to come here and apologise in some meaningless way.

Moira   I'm not asking you to apologise.

Dawn   That's very generous.

Moira   But then, I didn't ask you to come here.

Dawn   No.

Pause.

Dawn   So if you're not. Well. I mean what are you doing?

Moira   Happily employed . . . with something else.

Dawn   Yes but what?

Moira   Does that matter?

Dawn   No. Not if you don't want to talk about it.

Moira   It's not a secret.

Dawn   Never mind.

Moira   I run a little charity.

Dawn   Great.

Moira   It's OK.

Dawn   So kind of not that different.

Moira   I suppose.

Dawn   Excellent.

Moira   It pays the bills.

Dawn   Cool.

Pause.

Dawn   I'm going to have to pay bills.

Moira   You get used to it.

Dawn   I've forgotten all that.

Moira   It'll come back.

Dawn   But what if it doesn't?

Moira   It will.

Dawn   I'm scared.

Moira   We're all scared.

Dawn   Not like me.

Moira   Dawn. It'll be fine.

Dawn *starts to cry. She sobs quietly.* **Moira** *watches her but does not move to comfort.*

Dawn   I'm sorry.

Moira   Don't be.

Dawn   I come to your house and . . . and . . .

Moira   Don't feel bad.

Dawn   I must be crazy.

Moira   You're here now. Enjoy your coffee.

Peaceful silence.

Dawn   I remember everything that happened. Like it's burned on to my eyes. And at the same time I feel like I've forgotten all the important things. All the things that help you to get through. All the skills that people have. People just living. All of those things. I'm at the beginning again. But with even less . . . confidence than before. That's why I found you. I knew you'd know something. I knew you'd be able to tell me something about how to do it. How to start doing it. Because you were so good at that. Before I wrecked it all.

Pause.

Moira   I have no special knowledge.

Dawn   Not special. Not like a secret or anything. But explaining.

Moira   Explaining?

Dawn   Yes, making it seem possible.

Moira   Why wouldn't it be possible?

Dawn   Because it's all overwhelming.

Moira   And they didn't put you in touch, link you up with anyone?

Dawn   They gave me some phone numbers.

Moira   That's all?

Dawn   That's all.

Moira   What about at the hostel?

Dawn   They don't like me.

Moira   You said it's been three days.

Dawn   But they don't.

Moira   That's your perception. Which is too harsh on yourself. They behave the way they behave with everyone. You just have to get used to them. They know nothing about you. And by being there for a while they'll relax towards you and you'll do the same.

Dawn   How can you be sure?

Moira   I can't be sure. But it seems like a reasonable interpretation. It's much more reasonable than that they don't like you. They have no opinion of you at the moment, that's why they seem cold. But when they see that you're no trouble and you co-operate, then they will like you.

Dawn   Yes. Yes you're right.

Moira   You're feeling overwhelmed because everything has changed and all at once. You're pitched into a new world, which is not the same as the world you remember. But you're adaptable.

Dawn   I don't know that I am.

Moira But I do know that you are.

Dawn How?

Moira Because you adapted to the world you've come from. It was all new and terrifying once. But you got used to it. Now here's another test. But you have all you need to get by already in your own experience.

Pause.

Dawn That's good. Like deep breathing. Listening to you is like deep breathing. Calming.

Moira It's just common sense.

Dawn No it's . . . it's more than that.

Moira Not really.

Dawn But it doesn't make sense unless you say it.

Moira Dawn I have to stop trying to fix things, people and situations that are way beyond my control. I was . . . defeated by my . . . desire to help.

Pause.

Dawn I can't do it on my own.

Moira You've been on your own.

Dawn That's different.

Moira I disagree.

Dawn But you've never been there.

Moira I can still tell.

Dawn That's not fair.

Moira I'm just trying to prove to you that you're stronger than you think you are.

Dawn I'm just trying to say that it is much more complicated. I survived because, yes, because I had to, yes, but also because, everything . . . everything is so much more simple. And now suddenly it is much more complicated

again. And that's why I can't . . . and that's why I need
someone . . . and the only person who ever. Who ever. Is
you. And I should have done more to try and help you too.
You know, when I could. But even so you're the only person.
I'm sorry. I'm really sorry. But it's true.

Pause.

Moira   Isn't it much too early to tell?

Dawn   Desperation Moira. It concentrates the mind.

Moira   You need time. To test yourself.

Dawn   So are you saying no?

Moira   I don't know what the question is.

Dawn   Sure you do.

Moira   Say it.

Dawn   Please Moira.

Moira   Say it anyway.

Dawn   Be there for me.

Pause.

Moira   I can't.

Pause.

Dawn   You mean you won't.

Moira   Well whichever way. I can't.

Dawn   You wouldn't throw a lifeline to a drowning woman?

Moira   I don't think that's a good way of describing it.

Pause.

Dawn   Fine.

Moira   Dawn think about it. What you are asking is not
reasonable.

Dawn   Not reasonable.

Moira No.

Pause.

Dawn Fuck you.

Moira Dawn.

Dawn Fuck you.

Moira That's so unfair.

Dawn Oh yes, you'd know all about unfair wouldn't you.

Moira If you're going to insult me then you'd better leave.

Dawn What's the matter with you people?

Moira What does that mean?

Dawn With your training and your listening and your reflecting and your empowerment and your support. It's all to stop you getting close, to stop you caring beyond five o'clock. None of it is real.

Moira It can never be the same as friendship.

Dawn Friendship? There is no, no touching, no really getting into someone else's world.

Moira Maybe that's true most of the time. But in our case I'd say the boundaries were not observed in an advisable way.

Dawn Is that what they told you?

Moira Oh they didn't tell me anything.

Dawn You always put words in the way don't you. And you're always telling people what they're really thinking or really feeling.

Moira Why are we talking about the past?

Dawn Because you've fucking closed the door on the present. That's why.

Moira   I'm not trying to make you feel bad. I'm being straight with you.

Dawn   I've asked you for something.

Moira   Which I am not in a position to give.

Dawn   Jesus, I'm not asking to borrow money.

Moira   It's like you expected me to be there, waiting, for when you came out.

Dawn   No. No, that's not what I'm saying.

Pause.

Moira   Dawn. I want you to do well. I want you to thrive and to find a lot of happiness. I sincerely want that. But I'm not strong enough to be dragged back into the past. I can't deal with it.

Dawn   But you were . . . the best.

Moira   No. I failed.

Dawn   I never thought you failed.

Moira   That's kind. But I still can't.

Dawn   You understood everything.

Moira   I thought us people were all the same.

Dawn   I was just lashing out.

Moira   Yes. Lashing out.

Dawn   Don't look at me as if I'm a piece of shit.

Pause.

You fucking bitch.

Pause.

Help me.

Pause.

Fucking help me you fucking cunt.

Pause.

Why won't you fucking help?

Pause.

Why?

Pause.

Moira   Because you ruined my life.

Silence.

INTERVIEW

*A much younger **Moira** is being interviewed for a job. We see only her.*

Moira   OK, so why am I the best person for the job? Well . . .

Long pause.

Sorry. Well I don't know that I'm the best person. But . . . although I've just qualified I have experience. Not professional experience but from life. And also I have worked with children and families as a volunteer for a learning disability charity. So I've seen how challenging being a parent can be. I had my final placement in a busy duty team so I know the kinds of referrals that get made. But I think you either come into this by accident or somehow you're drawn, or maybe forced, if that's not too strong a word, yes, I think maybe, forced into considering social work because of the way your experience, as a young person, the way it shapes your thinking.

Pause.

It's like I knew I had to do something like social work because I watched things go . . . so wrong. I mean in my family. And I don't think that it's a wound you carry with you that you're seeking to heal by becoming a professional. I just think you have that knowledge, that pain, and you can use it, mine it, to help other people.

Pause.

I mean everyone is damaged. To some degree. But you either get stuck, fixating on the past or you do a deal with the future. It's not a terrible secret I have but just . . . such . . . unhappiness.

Pause.

Can I just have a moment? I know I should talk about the person spec and I did well on the course and I . . . I really want this job.

Pause.

I'm sorry . . .

Act Two

Prison visiting. **Dawn** *and* **Moira** *face each other across a table. Silence. Under the table* **Dawn** *holds a fork. She toys with it and then puts it up one of her sleeves. The audience notices this but* **Moira** *does not.*

Dawn   It's just that I didn't expect to see you.

Moira   Yes I know.

Dawn   I didn't expect to see anyone.

Moira   That's why I came.

Dawn   It's mad.

Moira   You're probably right.

Dawn   I mean won't you get . . . no?

Moira   Nobody knows I'm here.

Dawn   I didn't think they'd let you.

Moira   And I was surprised you accepted.

Dawn   Amazing isn't it? I get a choice.

Moira   You're on remand. They have to give you a choice.

Dawn   I'm not fighting it. I've decided what's the point.

Moira   I think that's wise.

Dawn   So what have they done with you?

Moira   I don't want to talk about that. That's not why I'm here.

Pause.

Dawn   OK.

Moira   Did they ask you about what happened?

Dawn   Yes sure.

Moira   Did you have to tell them about me?

Dawn   They asked a lot.

Moira   Of course.

Pause.

Moira   Look, I want to know you're going to get through. I want you to promise me.

Dawn   Why?

Moira   Because I know something about you.

Dawn   What do you know?

Moira   That what happened isn't . . . isn't all of you. That there are things that no one wants to accept now. That there are good things. About you. And that you need to hear them. As well as all the . . . damnation.

Pause.

Dawn   Good things?

Moira   Yes.

Dawn   You know I think that you lead a fantasy life Moira.

Moira   Oh.

Dawn   Yeah. A fantasy life in which you save everyone. Save everyone from themselves.

Moira   You wouldn't be the first to say that.

Dawn   I've been thinking about you.

Moira   I don't want to make things worse.

Dawn   Wondering about you.

Moira   I'll go if you want.

Dawn   Wondering what goes on in your head to make you hang around people like me.

Pause.

Moira   It's my job.

Dawn   You've still got a job have you?

Moira   No.

Pause.

Dawn   That's too bad.

Moira   It's not final yet. But the word is . . . no chance.

Dawn   I'm sorry.

Moira   If maybe you'd told them, I don't know, something positive.

Dawn   I didn't say anything bad.

Moira   Probably makes no difference.

Dawn   Sorry.

Moira   It's just bad luck.

Dawn   Bad fucking luck?

Moira   Well, I've got to tell myself something.

Pause.

Dawn   Sure. Know what you mean.

Moira   Whatever happens, you have to try and make sense of it.

Dawn   Why don't you hate me?

Moira   What good would that do?

Dawn   Why don't you hate me Moira?

Moira   There's been enough hatred.

Dawn   I don't believe you.

Pause.

Moira   Everything that happens . . . could happen to anyone. All the feelings are feelings that everyone has. That doesn't make things right. That doesn't excuse what you did. But we have to accept that . . . these things are in all of us.

Dawn   What a load of shit.

Moira   No, it's true.

Dawn   You're so fucked up.

Moira   You're just believing what authority has told you because judgment has been passed.

Dawn   I'm evil Moira.

Moira   I don't believe that for a minute.

Dawn   You're so fucking deluded.

Moira   And you're so full of self-loathing right now you'd accept anything bad that anyone says about you.

Dawn   I'm filth and you can't see it.

Moira   I don't think anyone is filth.

Dawn   You'd have been a fucking missionary. You'd have been force feeding the fucking Bible to Pigmies a hundred years ago.

Moira   Maybe.

Dawn   I'm locked up and the world is a safer place.

Moira   Really? Who are you a threat to?

Dawn   I'm disgusting. I should have been sterilised.

Pause.

Moira   I want you to promise me something.

Dawn   No way.

Moira   I'm serious.

Dawn   You can't trust any promise I'd make.

Moira   I want you to promise that you're not going to harm yourself.

Dawn   I don't do that crap.

Moira   Yes but Dawn, this is a university of stupidity and violence. Half the girls have got razors stuffed up their cunts.

Pause.

Dawn   I love it when you talk dirty.

Moira   Someone's going to slash herself in front of you. Someone is going to hang. And you must not think that's a good idea. Ever.

Dawn   Keeping me alive is a waste of taxpayers' money.

Moira   Will you promise?

Dawn   Don't believe in me Moira.

Moira   I'm not going until you promise.

Dawn   What does it matter?

Moira   It matters to me.

Dawn   Because you're twisted.

Moira   No.

Dawn   The thing about suicide is that it's such a neat ending.

Moira   Of course.

Dawn   Do you think I've got the energy to fight against what everyone thinks of me?

Moira   Yes I do.

Dawn   Don't take offence.

Moira   At what?

Dawn   It's for your own good.

Moira   What is?

Dawn   And don't cry out?

Moira   What are you talking about?

Dawn *slaps* **Moira** *hard across the face.*

Dawn   You're mad. Stop it.

Moira   That hurt.

Dawn   It's your wake-up call.

Moira   I'll just come back again.

Dawn   Christ.

Moira   Will you promise me?

Pause.

Dawn   I have no plans to kill myself.

Moira   But you will have. And I want you to promise that you won't act on them.

Dawn   I don't believe my own promises.

Moira   I just want you to promise me. Not anyone else. Me. That's all.

Dawn   No one in their right mind would be visiting me.

Moira   You need someone to visit you.

Dawn   Forget me. It's OK, I'll forget myself.

Moira   Promise me.

Dawn   But I'll only promise to make you go away.

Moira   Still, you will have promised.

Dawn   Ask me later.

Moira   I will.

Dawn   You know some people don't ever want to come out. I mean they're looking forward to not having to leave.

Moira   Sure.

Dawn   They can't get on out there. They keep coming back.

Moira   Are you like that?

Dawn   No. I'm not like anything. I just . . . need what I can't have. And if I get it I'll say I don't want it.

Moira   Like what?

Dawn   Do the maths Moira.

Pause.

Moira   Do you talk to people?

Dawn   Enough not to draw attention to myself.

Moira   So you have a strategy.

Dawn   I'm not ready to think.

Moira   Some of it's unconscious.

Dawn   Right.

Moira   There's things you'll need to learn, just to survive. But there's also . . .

Pause.

Dawn   Have you ever done time?

Moira   Me? No.

Dawn   Then what the fuck do you know?

Moira   I don't.

Dawn   But you talk like you do. Always. You talk like you've got this serene wisdom. But it's shit. There's something wrong with you. To want to come here.

Moira   Maybe.

Dawn   I'm worried about you.

Moira   Dawn don't just deflect.

Dawn   I'm worried what you'll do next.

Moira   Dawn.

Dawn   Isn't there a register or something? Some kind of list where they put down the names of bad people who might do something. You know, and everyone on that list has to be kept an eye on.

Pause.

Moira   You just need to know that someone at least out there is hoping for you to . . .

Dawn   Has to be paid a visit.

Moira   Hoping for you.

Dawn   Has to be kept under scrutiny. Under surveillance because they can't be trusted.

Pause.

Dawn   I think they should do that to you. Because you know what happens?

Moira   What happens?

Dawn   Sometimes you've just got to fulfil the expectations.

Moira   What expectations?

Dawn   Step up to the plate.

Moira   That's not what happened.

Dawn   And just do the worst fucking thing imaginable because they have already thought it of you.

Moira   I see.

Dawn   When they all say how shocked and disappointed they are they don't really mean it. In fact they love it. They love it when they know that deep down they've been right all along. They knew I was scum. They wanted me to be scum. And here I am, scum.

Moira   You'll get tired of thinking like this.

Pause.

Dawn   So are you going to redeem me?

Moira   No.

Dawn   I'm your biggest failure.

Moira   That's not how I look at it.

Dawn   I think you could try a little redemption.

Moira   You can mock me if you want but I'm not sure it's going to do that much for you.

Dawn   I never asked you to hope for me. Or to do anything for me. That's why it matters so much.

Moira   Does it?

Dawn   As long as I don't admit it.

Pause.

Dawn   But it's too late for me to be a better person.

Pause.

Dawn   I can't believe it's possible. But maybe you can?

Moira   Yes. Maybe.

Dawn   I can't live with myself long enough to speak without biting.

Moira   No.

Dawn   Do you understand?

Moira   Perhaps.

Dawn   It's why I slapped you.

Moira   I see.

Pause.

Dawn   I went into town once. Years ago. I was on the train and I noticed this couple. They had a kid who was asleep in a buggy. There was some kind of tension between them. I just picked up on it. They didn't say anything. But you could tell from the way they looked at each other that it wasn't so good. Anyway we came to my stop and I got up to leave. The bloke said something to the girl, something nasty, slag or bitch or something. And she got up to follow him. She didn't say anything but there was this look of desperation on her face. And the door opened and I waited for them to get off in front of me. And they did but they left the buggy behind them with the kid asleep. I couldn't believe it. You know, that they were so caught up with whatever shit was going on that they'd forgotten about this little sleeping kid. So I kind of froze. I looked at the buggy and I looked at them but they were walking on, well oblivious. I should have called out but I didn't think quickly enough. Anyway the doors of the train closed again and we started moving off. It was the sound of the train leaving that made the girl turn around. She suddenly spun around and looked at the train and I could see the realisation work its way across her features. Bloke or kid, bloke or kid, like a flashing light. And she ran towards the train and I managed to catch her eye. I pointed to the child and I mouthed the words 'next stop' at her. She nodded her head. So I went and sat down next to the buggy until the train stopped again. I should have pulled the alarm. That way the train stops even if it's only half in and half out of the station. But I was too slow. So I sat down and I looked at this kid, sleeping. He was a bit restless but otherwise he had no idea. And the train eventually came to a stop and I pushed the buggy off. What was strange was that no one else on the train seemed to have noticed a thing. And when I pushed the buggy off the train no one cared that I wasn't the mother, I was a stranger.

Pause.

So I waited. I sat down and the kid woke up because he felt the breeze on his face. And wasn't that surprised. He didn't cry or anything. So I started talking to him. I guess he was about three, maybe a bit more. And he was quite relaxed and friendly. He wasn't worried.

Pause.

And the next train pulled into the station and I thought, right here we go. And I watched everyone get off the train but the girl wasn't there. The train moved off again and I waited for everyone to walk past and out of the station. I couldn't believe it. She wasn't there. She hadn't come. So there was nothing else to do really but wait until the next train came. So we chatted away and he started to get a little worried but I was able to calm him down. And after a time the next train came. But the same thing happened. Nothing. No one. Where was she? Where was her bloke?

Pause.

So the third train pulled in. And just before it did I was overcome with this incredible sense of rage. I was disgusted. I didn't think it possible. How could anyone abandon their child like that? Their beautiful happy little child? The train came in and I thought to myself, I thought, you're too late. You're too late you stupid little tart. You're too fucking late. And just as the train was coming into the platform I pushed the boy in his buggy. I pushed him right over the edge of the platform as the train came in.

Pause.

Because that's the kind of person I am. That's the kind of thing I do.

Pause.

I thought of doing that. I really did. I thought it for about half a second. Because I thought, where are you? Where the fuck are you? And, well, who knows? Who knows where they were? So I sat there with the child. One train after another until we could be absolutely sure that they would not be coming. And then I took him to the police. Handed him over, like lost property. And he didn't want to go. It wasn't surprising. He cried and he tried to hang on to me. The police thought I was his mother and made me give them all my details. And I left the police station with the sound of his sobbing in my ears.

Pause.

Moira   Is that true? The right thing.

Dawn   Yes. The right thing.

Moira   Which is why?

Dawn   We all have hours of newsreel of ourselves being good, or at least not being bad and all it amounts to is time that has faded away.

Pause.

Dawn   You can't prove anything to me. There's nothing left.

Moira   I know that's how you feel.

Dawn   Except eyes. My eyes, they follow things. I notice things. But I don't feel. Not any more.

Moira   All the fuss will die down. The story will get forgotten, or replaced with the next one. Then you won't be known any more.

Pause.

Dawn   Did you let me down?

Moira   Did I?

Dawn Is that why it happened? That you let me down?

Moira Is that what you told them?

Dawn No.

Moira You didn't tell them anything.

Dawn I didn't write you a fucking reference no.

Moira OK, I'm sorry.

Dawn That's the only reason you're here isn't it.

Moira No. It's not.

Dawn Fuck.

Pause.

Moira It's just a visit.

Dawn To make you feel better about yourself.

Moira To see how you are.

Dawn To save yourself.

Moira To see how you are.

Dawn How am I?

Moira In the circumstances, not too bad.

Dawn So you've got what you want.

Pause.

Moira Have you heard from your mum?

Dawn No.

Moira Are you still in touch?

Dawn No.

Moira Would you like me to contact her?

Dawn No.

Moira   I don't mind.

Dawn   I do.

Moira   OK.

Dawn   I mind.

Moira   Fair enough.

Dawn   Why are you so fucking insistent?

Moira   I thought it might be something I could help with.

Dawn   Moira I just want to crawl back under the stone.

Moira   I wouldn't do anything unless you asked me to.

Dawn   Well that's not fucking true.

Moira   Yes it is.

Dawn   Oh maybe now that I'm in a cage.

Moira   Please stop attacking me.

Dawn   But before I was in a cage you would do anything you thought was in my best interests, which meant anything you thought was in your best interests.

Moira   Dawn.

Dawn   Because I don't actually have a voice.

Moira   How so?

Dawn   Because people like you. No, actually just you, are always speaking for me.

Moira   I'm not.

Dawn   And my voice gets drowned out by the noise of all your agonising.

Pause.

Dawn   Yeah, truth.

Moira   It's not the truth.

Dawn I could slap you all day and you wouldn't flinch.

Moira I don't have any feelings Dawn.

Dawn Am I supposed to care?

Moira Professionals don't have any feelings.

Dawn Thin-skinned, aren't you. Professionals seem to need so much more approval than their clients.

Moira Your life hasn't affected me at all.

Dawn You should see someone.

Moira I should think about the future.

Dawn See someone and talk. Get it off your chest.

Moira Didn't that ever help?

Dawn It made you feel better.

Moira Would silence have been better?

Dawn I had no choice.

Moira You needed help.

Dawn So you keep saying.

Moira And you did talk.

Dawn Is that what happened?

Moira And we made progress.

Dawn We?

Moira Yes.

Dawn You put your hand down my throat and pulled out my guts.

Moira And if I hadn't ?

Dawn Then everything would be perfect.

Moira Of course.

Dawn   I served my function. The caring services have moved on to care for someone else.

Moira   Shall I come again?

Dawn   Yes. And no. So no.

Moira   And if you change your mind?

Dawn   I always change my mind. It's not in my nature to be consistent.

Moira   So I won't come.

Dawn   I can't make the decision for you.

Moira   Alright.

Dawn   I'm sorry.

Pause. **Dawn** *gently touches* **Moira**'s *face.*

Moira   You take care then.

Dawn   Take care of what?

Moira   Will you promise me you won't harm yourself?

Dawn   What if I do harm myself, what will you do?

Moira   I won't be here, I won't be able to do anything.

Dawn   But what would you do?

Moira   I'd try to stop you.

Dawn   Would you?

Moira   Of course.

Dawn   Then what?

Moira   Then I'd try to find out why you did it.

Dawn   You wouldn't be quick enough to stop me. And you'd be too shocked to ask me why.

Moira   That's just one more thing for us to disagree about.

Dawn   Goodbye Moira.

Pause

Moira   Goodbye Dawn.

Pause. **Moira** *stands up. As she does so* **Dawn** *lets the fork fall from her sleeve which she takes up and plunges into the back of her other hand which is on the table.*

Moira   Oh my God. Oh Jesus.

Dawn   Do you still care about me now?

Moira *is completely confused. Fade.*

ENQUIRY

Dawn *speaks. She is speaking to an official of some kind whom we do not see.*

Dawn   Yes it may be unusual. Yes, but I wanted to say something. I mean I changed my mind. Yes it's too late and all that but it's not about me you see. I wanted to say that she was good. You know, a very good social worker. Obviously coming from me that may seem a bit odd. But this shouldn't have any consequences for her is what I'm saying. Yes. That's what I'm saying. So if decisions have been made. If any action or punishment or whatever. I think it's unfair. I couldn't say it before. It's not that I didn't want to, it's just that I couldn't think. I couldn't move my mind at all. I don't expect anything. But you're always taking notes. Nothing is ever not on the record. So I don't see why. I mean my version must count for something here. It must. I mean thank you for seeing me. Will you pass it on? Will you make it official? I mean if you can? To whoever.

Pause.

Will you?

Act Three

The threshold of **Dawn***'s home.* **Moira** *and* **Dawn** *face each other. Long silence.*

Dawn   You again.

Moira   Can I come in?

Dawn   Why?

Moira   Well, I need to see you.

Dawn   Here I am. You can see me.

Moira   No, I need to see your home.

Dawn   What's wrong with my home?

Moira   I need to see Amy.

Dawn   She's asleep.

Moira   That's OK, I'll wait.

Dawn   Wait for what?

Moira   Until she wakes up.

Dawn   She didn't sleep well last night. She's very tired.

Moira   Why didn't she sleep?

Dawn   I don't know.

Moira   Can I come in then?

Dawn   I'd prefer if you didn't.

Moira   I'm afraid it's my job.

Dawn   What, forcing your way into people's homes?

Moira   I've no intention of forcing my way in.

Dawn   What gives you the right?

Moira   The law.

Dawn   What law says you can come in here?

Moira   The local authority has a duty to protect children and to help parents who may be struggling.

Dawn   I'm managing fine.

Moira   I'm sure you are and I just want to help you.

Dawn   You know that's what loan sharks say. In the beginning.

Moira   But I'm not a loan shark.

Dawn   No, you're worse.

Moira   Well, let's see if I can change your mind.

Pause. **Dawn** *steps aside so that* **Moira** *can come in. There is a carry cot in the corner of the room.*

Dawn   Let's just talk quietly then.

Moira   OK.

Pause.

Moira   So how is she?

Dawn   She's fine. She's well.

Moira   And what about you?

Dawn   I'm good.

Moira   No stress?

Dawn   Everyone has stress. So what?

Moira   It's a very new experience though.

Dawn   What is?

Moira   Having a baby.

Dawn   People have been having babies for millions of years.

Moira   Yes, but it's still a huge change.

Dawn   She's OK.

Moira   So you feel positive about things.

Dawn   I feel . . .

Pause.

Moira   Yes?

Dawn   I feel . . . relief.

Moira   Oh.

Dawn   Yes. That it's going to be OK. That I'm going to cope.

Moira   That's great.

Dawn   I thought I might not. But I will. I'll be fine.

Pause.

Moira   Is she keeping you up at night?

Dawn   Sometimes.

Moira   It's very tiring isn't it.

Dawn   Do you have children?

Moira   No. No I don't.

Dawn   So how come you're such an expert then?

Moira   I'm not an expert.

Dawn   Do you not think it would be a good idea, like a qualification, that you had to have kids of your own before you go judging how other people do it?

Moira   I'm not judging.

Dawn   People like me can't be trusted to breed. That's what you think.

Moira   You do that a lot.

Dawn   Do what?

Moira You tell me what I'm thinking.

Dawn Do you think you've lived?

Moira Of course I've lived.

Dawn Seen it all have you?

Pause.

Moira I'm not comparing myself with you. There are things you've seen and done that I will never experience.

Dawn What, vicious council trash experience you mean.

Moira No. I only mean that you know lots of things I don't know. So I'm not trying to say I'm better in any way.

Dawn Only rich women get to be bad mothers unsupervised.

Moira We're not the enemy.

Dawn We're not going to be friends.

Moira Maybe not. But we can get along.

Dawn What do I have to do to make you fuck off? Sign her up for private school?

Pause.

Moira Social workers are trained Dawn. I had to work hard. I went to university. We studied psychology, social policy and the history of social work. We looked at the theories behind the interventions that are made. We had to go on placements in different teams. And then when you get a job you build up experience; and you have supervision and team meetings to discuss what's happening. It's not random, it's not prying; it's considered and planned.

Dawn Well aren't you lucky.

Pause.

Moira I'd resent me too, if I were you.

Dawn   Sure.

Moira   But what I'd do is I'd co-operate and I'd put me at ease and then Moira would fuck off much sooner.

Dawn   Play the game.

Moira   It's not a game.

Dawn   Isn't that what you just said?

Moira   You can do what we want grudgingly and I would understand that. But I believe it's important. You might get away with thinking it's a game but I won't.

Dawn   What's that? Iron fist in a velvet glove?

Moira   We've been worried because you've had real problems. Those were all your own business until you had Amy. But now that Amy is here, we need to know that you can look after her, and love her, and care for her and nurture her, and let her thrive. Not because we don't trust you but because that's what every child deserves.

Dawn   Don't I have a right to try all that without the fucking police questioning me every step of the way? Health visitors, social workers, case conferences, planning meetings.

Moira   It's a process and it's there to make sure we all think about you as an individual and look at your particular needs, and what's best for Amy. It's a supportive process. It can seem oppressive. But what we want to do is to help you to survive with Amy, by getting to the point where no one is worried about you. Not to make things perfect, but to make things good enough.

Pause.

Moira   But I know you've had a really hard time, I know.

Dawn   You're not better than me. But everything you say implies you're better than me.

Moira I'm not better than you. And it's not fair. I'm much more privileged. And I know it all seems patronising.

Dawn You have no idea.

Moira But it's not just about you. It's about Amy.

Dawn I gave birth to Amy, not you. I carried Amy. I protected her through all . . .

Pause.

Moira Yes you did.

Dawn Through all the . . . shit.

Moira Absolutely, and I could never have done that.

Pause.

Moira Because I'm nowhere near as strong as you.

Dawn Fuck off.

Moira I'm trying to do something practical, to make life better for the people I work with. By building on their strengths and their potential.

Dawn I just want you to go away.

Moira I know.

Dawn I can't prove I can be trusted.

Moira Of course you can.

Dawn Really?

Moira Yes really.

Dawn What, even with crack whore written on the front of the file?

Moira Dawn, if we didn't think you could do it then we wouldn't have let you keep her in the first place.

Dawn You'd have taken her after I'd given birth?

Moira   It happens all the time.

Dawn   And what happens to the poor bitches?

Moira   The poor bitches find some way to survive.

Pause.

Dawn   So let's say you did have a kid.

Moira   OK.

Dawn   Who would be judging you?

Moira   The same rules apply to me.

Dawn   No, no. Who's going to start it all?

Moira   Well, if I came to the attention of social services.

Dawn   How did I come to your attention?

Moira   Your GP. Pre-natal.

Dawn   Fuck, the police are everywhere. With their opinions.

Moira   It was an observation not an opinion.

Dawn   Same thing.

Moira   I disagree. There was some objectivity.

Dawn   Whatever.

Pause.

Dawn   So who would start? Who would question you?

Moira   If I wasn't coping.

Dawn   No one would start. No one Moira. Ever. You'd be free to make your mistakes.

Moira   I'd get the benefit of the doubt I suppose.

Dawn   It's like pre-pay meters.

Moira   What?

Dawn   If you need one they make you pay more. You pay more for your gas than millionaires.

Moira   If you say so.

Dawn   I mean I don't get the same chance.

Moira   No you're right. You are right. It's not just. And society is not just. But I only want to help you to manage the stress of being a new parent. And I only want to keep an eye on you until Amy is doing well and we can go and annoy someone else.

Dawn   OK.

Moira   You can make me an ally.

Dawn   You're not the worst stuck-up tart I've ever met.

Moira   Is that a compliment?

Dawn   I wouldn't go that far.

Moira   You seem more, I don't know, angry than usual. Has anything happened?

Pause.

Dawn   I wouldn't want to do your job.

Moira   It's not that bad.

Dawn   Why do you do it?

Moira   Because I'm good at it.

Dawn   That's not the whole reason.

Moira   Well, it's more complicated obviously.

Dawn   What are you guilty about?

Moira   I'm not guilty.

Dawn   You're trying to make up for something.

Moira   Am I now?

Dawn   Something you've done. Or maybe something you haven't done.

Moira   Why?

Dawn   I'm your guilt. I'm your Hail fucking Mary.

Moira   I wanted to do something that was worth it. You know, a job that wasn't just about making money, or making something crap that I had to pretend was valuable.

Dawn   You were talking to yourself.

Moira   What do you mean?

Dawn   Worthy people. You're just showing off to yourself.

Moira   So it's not worth doing?

Dawn   I don't know. But who elected you to save the world?

Moira   My family wasn't so great. There were problems. Divorce and alcohol and . . . Look, it's not guilt that made me a social worker but . . . living with those issues. I mean I had to think about how people survive . . . and how they change.

Pause.

Moira   Is helping you such a bad thing?

Dawn   I'm sure it's very noble.

Moira   Social work is not charity. It's a job. It's a vocation. A fucking difficult one. But you know what? I'm sticking with it. I'm sticking with you.

Dawn   You think you can change someone after twenty-five years?

Moira   Maybe. But Amy isn't twenty-five.

Dawn   No.

Moira   So she needs things to be a bit different.

Pause.

Dawn   So give me fifty grand and I'll be good.

Moira   You'd bring up your child if we paid you?

Dawn   If I tell you the truth you either don't believe me or you don't like it. If I lie, well, it's exactly the same. I can never win.

Moira   Has something happened?

Dawn   Nothing you wouldn't expect.

Pause.

Moira   Dawn, when you found out you were pregnant, what did you think?

Dawn   I thought flush it quick.

Moira   No you didn't.

Dawn   You're right. I thought about the sacredness of life and the glory of God's gift.

Pause.

Dawn   You're the priest, you're the police.

Moira   Why can't you talk to me?

Dawn   I am talking to you.

Pause.

Moira   Why did you call her Amy?

Dawn   Amy was my best friend at school.

Moira   Does she know you called your child after her?

Dawn   No.

Moira   Maybe she should.

Dawn   She's gone from my life. She . . . had to go.

Moira   I don't understand.

Dawn   She put in for an early exit.

Moira   She killed herself?

Dawn   Spot on.

Pause.

Moira   Well it's a lovely way to commemorate a friend.

Dawn   Yeah.

Moira   How long ago?

Dawn   Last year.

Moira   Did you . . . did you find her?

Dawn   No. She went away. Spain.

Moira   Oh.

Dawn   Very tasteful. Hung herself from an olive tree.

Moira   I'm sorry.

Dawn   She loved a drama.

Moira   Well . . .

Dawn   She was probably hoping the branch would break.

Moira   How old was she?

Dawn   Same as me. Silly bitch.

Pause.

Dawn   She was a good laugh.

Moira   I'm sorry.

Dawn   She just did whatever came into her head. Like, suicide, that'd be fun, let's do it. And we'd all, they'd all be going like yes, go for it girl. And she'd be mad. And drunk. And then fuck. I don't know what happened. I wish I'd been there. I could have clapped and then cut her down.

Moira   So you miss her?

Dawn *nods.*

Moira   What was it like for you when you were growing up?

Dawn   You mean did I have enough love?

Moira   I suppose.

Dawn   Join the dots and you'll get to my soul.

Moira   I've only got a few things to say. I just have to say them over and over. We want to help. We have a duty to watch out for Amy. I think you and I can work together. That's all I'm about.

Dawn   My mother. It wasn't her fault that I turned out like a filthy pair of knickers. It wasn't her fault. I love her because she's my mum, I hate her because she's my mum. That's all I can do. You see, if I tell you anything it makes me so much more understandable and so much less individual. Doesn't it? You know things about me and then I'm less. Everything you know about me makes me disappear.

Moira   No. It helps me to see you more clearly.

Pause.

Dawn   My friend Jean, well not my friend really, but some other mother on the estate, she told me, that they'll seduce you into co-operation. That's what she said. The best of them don't use fear. They seduce you.

Moira   I've never looked at it that way.

Dawn   You can't love her for me. Amy. You can't love her for me.

Moira   Of course I can't.

Dawn   But that's what you want to be able to do. That's why you exist.

Moira   No.

Dawn   People have got pride Moira.

Moira   I know.

Dawn   My father had his pride.

Moira   Yes.

Dawn   So they say.

Moira   He died when you were young.

Dawn   He was killed.

Moira   Was he.

Dawn   But before they killed him, they cut his face off with a breadknife.

Moira   Christ Dawn that's terrible.

Dawn   Just one of those things.

Moira   Your father.

Dawn   Shit happens.

Moira   Oh my God.

Dawn   He was dealing on their patch. Had it coming.

Moira   You can't think that.

Dawn   Business is business.

Moira   No.

Dawn   But he didn't scream. Totally silent. Must have been his pride.

Moira   Christ.

Dawn   Actually he died of liver failure. He was an alcoholic.

Moira   Was he?

Dawn   No, he died of Huntington's disease. It was horrible watching him waste away.

Moira   Dawn.

Dawn   To be honest he didn't die at all. He's alive and well and living in Cleethorpes.

Moira   Well.

Pause.

Dawn   Each time you make a different judgement.

Moira   I just want to know the truth.

Dawn   Yes exactly, so you can draw your conclusions about how what happened made me the fuck-up I am.

Moira   I'm not saying you're a fuck-up at all.

Dawn   Only fuck-ups have social workers Moira. Think of your caseload. Fuck-ups numbers 1 to 15.

Pause.

Moira   You're responsible for your choices Dawn but upbringing still affects the way you turn out.

Dawn   Do we turn out? Is that the only option? I haven't turned out yet. I'm still in the process of being fucked up. You've got to wait until it's finished.

Moira   If I know about your parents and how you were raised it will tell me a lot, that's not being overly deterministic, it's just common sense.

Dawn   Did I have a choice?

Moira   How do you mean?

Dawn   Did I have a choice about my parents?

Moira   Obviously not.

Dawn   So am I to blame?

Moira   To blame for what?

Dawn   For my personality, for my behaviour?

Moira   Well everyone is responsible for their behaviour.

Dawn   Then why will you learn anything by knowing about my parents?

Moira   People always have choices and they are always responsible but the choices they have are shaped by their upbringing, by their environment. It's not equal or fair.

Dawn   Did you have a choice?

Moira   A choice about what?

Dawn   A choice about social work. Or was it destiny?

Moira   Of course I had a choice.

Dawn   Maybe you didn't. Maybe you're a victim. Don't you want to be a victim?

Moira   No.

Dawn   It's much easier that way. Victims deserve understanding.

Moira   But a victim of what?

Dawn   Disadvantage. Brutality.

Moira   What brutality?

Dawn   My parents kept me in a cage in the living room and fed me only raw meat. I didn't learn to talk until I was eighteen.

Moira *stands up.*

Moira   Enough. Enough.

Pause.

Moira   Have it your way. We speak like adults, I treat you with respect or I come back with other people, I do visits with the police and with a manager because you won't co-operate. We can take Amy away Dawn.

Dawn *stares at her. She makes a decision.*

Dawn   OK I'm sorry.

Moira   I have to go anyway.

Dawn   No don't go. Don't go.

Moira *is still standing.*

Dawn I've no one to . . . I mean it's good, it helps. To talk.
Please.

Moira *sits down. Pause*

Dawn Look I just have to . . . can you listen to me? I mean
can you wait . . . and listen?

Moira Yes.

Pause.

Dawn Because something has happened. OK.

Moira I'm listening.

Dawn OK. The truth OK? The whole truth and
nothing but?

Pause.

Dawn OK?

Moira OK.

Pause.

Dawn So I had Amy. I gave birth to Amy. I carried her
around, I thought about her, felt her growing, named her.
I couldn't believe she was mine. You know, when she was
born, I couldn't believe. I mean in a good way. I was scared
but I was grateful. No, I was overwhelmed. It was, the
feelings, they were exactly what you hope. Like I was doing
it by the book, but without having to force anything. The
love, the feeling of being amazed. I didn't have to fake it. I'd
faked a lot of feelings before. I'd told people I loved them
when I didn't. Pretended to be a friend when I wasn't. I'd
done a lot of that, so I was afraid that when it really mattered
that I feel something genuine, that I would be empty. That
I'd have to try, to work at what should be natural. But it was.
That was good. That was very good. I began to think that
I might not be worthless after all. Because I could hold her

and everything was possible and all that shit. When hope, you know, when optimism is just not something you're used to then, there's this kind of battle goes on inside you. A great new feeling and your cynicism. They have it out big time. But that was . . . those first weeks. No sleep, total fear but you get carried through don't you. And I suppose that strength that comes from nowhere, I suppose that's what convinced you bastards. You know, to let me go home. The new me. Coping. Making a go of it. That baby will be the making of her. Who'd have thought. The turnaround. Yeah.

Pause.

But it's not easy. And you start to wonder. Doubt is also a very strong thing. You can deal with the short term, the early stuff, that's OK. But it's going to go on isn't it. It's going to go on and on and on. And you wonder about your own stamina. Each little battle with yourself counts for nothing really. Because you know what the long run is like. The inner belief. I've always let myself down eventually. She's so small. So utterly dependent. She cries a lot but you can deal with it because you can pick her up. She can't resist that, you can just pick her up and hold her and feed her and at last it will stop. Her crying. When it works, it's beautiful. You have this control. But often it doesn't work. Or at least it doesn't work as quickly as you want it to. When you're tired. When she reminds you, that you're the one who has responsibility. You could do anything to her. Anything at all.

Pause.

So, often you find yourself shouting. It's what we experience. First. Deepest. Not reason. Not calm. No. Shouting. That's how you get what you want. So you shout. At her. She cries and I shout. Shut up. Shut up now. Shut the fucking hell up now. And then it's done. Because it takes a little time for the realisation of how useless that is. It takes a little time for it to sink in. To overcome the anger. And the shame. And the fact that you have shouted at a powerless little baby.

Pause.

So the next time you don't shout. You shake. You shake
her. She cries and you shake her. And then you hug her.
You endanger and you embrace. Rage to love. We all feel it.
We may not all do it. I know most people are perfect. Most
people don't need parenting lessons or education in child
welfare. Most people don't do silly things. Just the scum. We
shout and we shake. And then we kiss and we cuddle. Then
we shout and we shake again. Because we don't learn. We
don't fucking learn.

Pause.

But that's not enough. Because it stops being about her
crying. All babies cry. Get over it. It's not enough. Because
you can make her cry. And you can make her stop. I love
her because she is every meaning. Everything good I could
be is her.

Pause.

So I had a cigarette. I smoke outside. I've seen the ads. But
she wanted me. And I was smoking my cigarette and she
wanted me. And I'm not really sure, honestly, not really sure
at all how this happens, how you go from here to there. How
you cross the line. But I put the tip of the cigarette against
her cheek. I held it there. And yes she cried louder and she
tried to turn her face away. But I dictate what happens. I
mean that's a given. I have control so I see what happens.
And I burned a little hole. And then oh. And then I pick her
up and I want the world to end. And I want not to be able
to do . . . anything. And I hold her and I soothe her and she
cries and I kiss her and I comfort her and the pain must ease
or something because she doesn't cry at all, she snuggles into
me and she breathes in and out. She is quiet.

Pause.

You test the power you have. You're drawn to do it. Because
she'll forgive anything. She forgives. Like I did. Like I

forgave. And you have to know. You have to know why.
Because kids love their parents. They love and they cannot
help loving. And they accept and they have the biggest
hearts in the universe. They love you when they hate you,
even though they hate you. They keep loving. So I have to
ask, what's the limit? What would she not forgive? Small and
beautiful and sleeping. What would she not forgive?

Pause.

My thoughts ran like this. Ran away with me. And I followed
them. That's what happened. I followed them without
question. I asked myself. I put a cigarette against her face.
We survive. What next? I boiled the kettle. I boiled the kettle
out of what? Was it curiosity? And I just let a small drop
fall on her face. The same small face I had already burned
with my cigarette. And one drop and two drops and then I
poured everything. On her little face. And I was thinking,
please stop me. Please cry. Please force me to think again.

Pause.

But she didn't. Of course. There was no sound. There was
no resistance. There was nothing. Except my understanding
. . . that there would be nothing. Ever.

Pause. **Moira** *gets up slowly and walks over to the carry cot. She
looks in and discovers the worst. She stands and looks at* **Dawn**.

Dawn   I wouldn't do that.

Pause.

I couldn't do something like that.

Pause.

It didn't happen.

End.

Printed in the USA
CPSIA information can be obtained
at www.ICGtesting.com
LVHW020940171024
794056LV00003B/872

9 781408 172674